TO DOUBT IS HUMAN

Chioma Egbuna

ISBN: 978-978-8415-92-3

Printed and published by:
Thinkers Publishers
P. O. Box 306 Agulu, Anambra State
E-mail: thinkerspublishing@gmail.com
Website: https://thinkerspublishers.business.site/
WhatsApp/Call: 08038393389, 08189979009

DEDICATION

To my boy, Neso-chukwu Valerian Chibuikem Egbuna.

I hope you read this book one day and know that God didn't give you to me to be perfect. He made you to be human.

ACKNOWLEDGMENTS

All Glory be to The Father, The Son and The Holy Spirit, as it was in the beginning, it is now and ever shall be, world without end, Amen.

Sir & Lady Chike E. Egbuna, my parents, thank you for nurturing and raising me.

Chinedu, Onyii and Amaka, my brother and my fierce and incredible sisters, thank you for the commitment, support, love and encouragement you've shown me. I am glad we are in each other's corner.

Nwa m, Neso-chukwu Valerian Egbuna, thank you for coming into my life. Like I always say, you are my son and I love you with all my heart.

My close friends and professional colleagues, Kingsley, Jane Frances and Chinomso, my school mates from F.G.G.C Onitsha and Nnamdi Azikiwe University, Ify Charles and Chioma Okafor, my big sister, Mrs. Stella Anyanwu and my friends, Ijeoma Ada Uche and Chisom Chidiebere, thank you for taking the time to read through the first draft. Thank you for the support, the reviews and constructive feedback. You gave me the confidence I needed to publish this book and I don't take your love and support for granted.

My friends from Facebook, thank you for your support and the constructive feedback you gave me when I posted the book covers on my wall and sought your view.

To you who will buy this book for yourself and your loved ones, and you who will encourage others to buy and read, thank you.

Chukwu gozielum unu.

God bless you all for me.

CONTENTS

DEDICATION iii

ACKNOWLEDGMENTS iv

REVIEWS viii

INTRODUCTION 1

CHAPTER ONE: Moments of Doubt 7

CHAPTER TWO: Simon Peter 19

CHAPTER THREE: Father of the Possessed 42

CHAPTER FOUR: Thomas 59

CHAPTER FIVE: God rewards doubt 78

REVIEWS

(What some readers said)

"I think it's a short, simple read that offers a fresh perspective on our relationship with ourselves and God."

Mrs. Onyinye Ugochukwu.
Legal Practitioner, Educator.

"Wow... the book is just so amazing. To start with, I don't normally read the introductory part of a book but the lines and story you used there forced me to read it to the end. It is written in simple language and easy to understand. Another wonderful thing about the book is that you used known disciples like Peter, John the Baptist and Thomas. I don't think there's anyone who haven't heard their stories. Using these known disciples makes the book relatable. I now understand what really happened to Thomas and if I'm being frank, I would do the same if I was in his shoes. Thank you Chioma for such a wonderful piece. It just seems like you were talking to me directly. To doubt is truly human. May

God meet each and every one of us at the point of our need... Amen."

Chisom Chidiebere
Entrepreneur, Founder SomSam Empire.

"To doubt is human, awesome topic. I must commend you for a work well done. We as humans cannot say that we have not at a certain time in our lives put up a doubt. For example, the time of my life that I has a miscarriage was the darkest and bad time of my life and I asked God series of questions. That could be seen as losing faith in God and doubting God. I asked those questions because I was in a lot of pain. I was shattered, confused and in doubt but it didn't make me less of a Christian. Likewise the same way you emphasized on your mom asking similar questions when fire ravaged her shop. It is indeed true that God can handle our doubts and unbelief. We won't also turn blind eyes to the doubting nature of man which is why indeed, to doubt is human. It is an interesting book including the stories from the bible and the bible verses .... Brilliant."

I.J
Entrepreneur.

"Sis, you really did a great job here. This book has lifted my spirit and I feel so relieved. I related all the Bible analysis with my personal experiences and I felt light within me. I love the way you and your friend analyzed the issues of doubt, confusion, regrets and shame using the story of Peter.... Ah! I learnt a lot of lessons dear. Your book is a great burden lifter. Your book and other stories from the bible you used have taken away confusion to an extent from my heart and brought this calmness and peace. I learnt that when we stay focused, reach out to God, cry out to Him for help, He will help and save us, plus give us the inner peace only Him can give. Thanks sis.

Ify Charles.

"Chy, this is awesome. I don't know a better adjective with which to qualify the book. This isn't to flatter you. One thing that thrills me is that you broke it down to what an ordinary man on the street can read and relate it with every aspect of his life. In simple terms, the book resonates with everyone out there and you didn't just tell us it's normal to have doubts but you broke it down to pieces as to what we can do in such situations. It's just so beautifully done. May God continually lift and be with you... Amen."

Chioma Doris.

"This book is wonderful, as in, I read the Bible and these passages you highlighted, especially the stories of Peter and John the Baptist but honestly, I never really saw their stories of doubts and I couldn't relate until I read this book. See how you broke down their stories and related them to the day-to-day human experiences. The analysis is flawless and there was no boring moment at all. You just gave us the permission to travel through your eyes and your thoughts."

Chinomso.

Legal Practitioner/Consultant.

"I sent you a voice note yesterday but I don't think I captured the awesomeness of this book. So, I decided to write and let you know that this book is great. I don't have adequate words with which to describe it. Apart from the fact that it is simple to read and understand, written in really 'down to earth' English, it is also very relatable. You outdid yourself this time. For everyone who appreciates self-care and self-improvement, I highly recommend this book."

Amaka

"This is a compelling life message! It is fit to be delivered on pulpits. I recommend it to many pastors who preach the gospel in a religious way instead of doing so in a living, realistic way. The book is a classic of a normal Christian living!

Kingsley

Legal Practitioner/Consultant.

INTRODUCTION

It was that time of the night and Sister Mary Clarence wasn't used to being in a room, not to talk of a cubicle with nothing but a narrow bed and a lamp. She was Deloris Van Catier, a Las Vegas show girl who had witnessed the murder perpetrated by her boyfriend.

Her boyfriend wasted no time to order his men to "waste her" and she had to seek asylum in a convent and become Sister

Mary Clarence. That night, she had said good night to Sister Mary Robert and a talking alarm clock was in her hand when she heard some noise.

She looked through her window and beheld a familiar sight.

Bubbling streets, youths dressed in denim jackets and shorts, and chatting heartily in twos and threes.

She rose from her bed and tip-toed out from the quiet and serene convent, to the street and into a bar. She endured the stares and the side comments as she walked to the man at the jukebox, put on her favourite track, talked with him a little and settled to her bottle of chilled coke.

Then she looked behind and saw them.

By "them", I mean Sister Mary Robert and Sister Mary Patrick.

"What were they doing in the bar? Wait! Did they follow her?"

Before she could say "What...", Sister Mary Patrick was with the man at the jukebox, and she selected and danced and twirled to "Gimme, Gimme, Gimme gravy tonight".

Sister Mary Clarence succeeded in dragging them away and they walked back to the convent in high spirits.

However, their high spirits were lowered when they walked into the Reverend Mother in the hallway and looked into her stern eyes.

Like most Nigerians would joke, "There was a caught".

Later that day, the Reverend Mother asked that "another suitable home" be found for Sister Mary Clarence.

Sister Mary Clarence apologized and reminded her of one of the virtues they were known for; Forgiveness, and the Reverend Mother made a statement that stuck with me.

"To err is human and to forgive is divine."

It was the first time I heard the statement and I remember that I asked my parents and my aunt what those clauses meant. I also took my time and conducted a little research, and from what I heard and discovered, it's a saying that reiterates the imperfect nature of man and the natural implication of being human.

Simply put, as humans, it is natural to err, to do the wrong things, to make poor choices and to commit blunders.

So when I racked my brain in search of a suitable title for this book, a title that will convey the exact message I want to deliver to you, I remembered the words I heard from the Reverend Mother in the movie, Sister Act. However, I decided to tweak it and let you know that contrary to whatever you've heard and were taught earlier, doubt is one of the natural implications of being human.

I also shared a conversation and an experience I had with a close friend in 2015 when my son was about 2 months old. In short, this book was inspired by the conversation and the experience I had with my friend that eventful Saturday morning and I hope that by the time you read the last line of this book, you'll agree with me that indeed, to doubt is human.

Let's do this.

CHAPTER ONE

Moments of Doubt

"We are most susceptible to doubt when the world weighs heavy on us"

- **Chris Carter.**

My mom used to trade at the popular Main Market Onitsha. This was years ago before she took up her teaching job.

I was in primary school then and my siblings and I had woken up one early morning and discovered that our parents were nowhere to be found. My aunt and our grown house help were there to help us get ready for school but as kids, we wondered where mom and dad had gone and why they weren't around when we left for school.

It turned out that Main Market Onitsha, one of the largest markets in West Africa, caught fire the previous night and was razed down, and not even one pin was salvaged. A lot of traders and Onitsha business men lost their goods which were worth millions of naira and a lot of them lost their shops.

My mom was among the business owners who lost their shops and when we returned in the evening, as much as she tried to be cheerful, her eyes were swollen and her voice had cracked.

It was even reported that one or two men jumped into the nearby River Niger and drowned because they felt that having lost their shops, there was nothing else to live for.

Truly, those were dark and tough days.

Some days after the incident, one of our family friends, a fair lady who was known as Mama Chidimma (Chidimma's mother) visited my mom. While they talked, my mom sobbed as she narrated her ordeal.

"God, where were you?" she asked. "People will die of hunger. Those shops, those goods were all people had. Those were all I had and you know exactly the financial state of my home. What do you want me to do now? How do I start afresh? Do I take it you knew this would happen yet you allowed me to make that bulk purchase so I could lose everything? Do I take it that you led me on, that you gave me a bag of salt and still sent the rain to meet me on my way out? Even if humans were responsible for this colossal damage, couldn't you have stopped them? You are powerful enough to stop them and prevent this so why didn't you?"

"Sssssshhhhh. Stop it."

It was Chidimma's mom.

"You speak like one who doesn't know God. Are you no longer a person of faith? What's the use of the Sunday Masses and other church activities you attend, and the faith you profess if you have to question God the way you just did?"

My mom continued to sob and shake her head.

"When this is over and you get back on your feet, you have to go for confession because you have sinned by questioning and doubting God."

I stood close to the door and I heard everything they discussed that evening, and most importantly, I learnt that one mustn't doubt or question God. I learnt it was a sin, that we must show unshakable faith in God at all times and that God would be angry if we lose faith and ask Him questions.

Many years later, everything I heard and learned that day was challenged and shaken to the core.

15 or 16 years later, I found myself holding my 2 months old baby and rubbing his back so as to get him to burp before laying him close to me on the sofa, in the three bedroom apartment I shared with my parents at Fegge, Onitsha.

A primary school classmate and childhood friend sat with me and I knew he watched as I tried to swim in the raging waters of single motherhood with my head just above the water. I deliberately avoided his eyes and pretended my son had all my attention.

"Chioma, you're doing so well with him and no matter what happens, I don't want you to ever doubt God's love for you."

I raised my face and met his gaze. He nodded in affirmation and I scoffed and shook my head.

"Stop it please or rather, tell me something I haven't heard. Listen, I'm not saying God doesn't love people. However, I know He can't possibly love someone like me who brought nothing but shame and disappointment to her family, the church, the entire womanhood and even herself. I've disgraced myself and my family. Do you even know how disappointed they are in me and how the mere sight of me disgusts them?"

It was my friend's turn to shake his head.

He was still for a few seconds and then he spoke.

"You know, I'm not going to blame you for everything you just said about you. I don't believe them but I won't blame you because I understand how you feel. All I ask is that you remember to go to God even in your doubts and with these hideous things you just said about yourself."

I remember that at this point, I thought to myself, "Okay. Now I think you need to leave."

Of course I didn't say it to him because well, he was my friend but I felt so irritated that I felt like pushing him out from my home.

"Remember to go to God in my doubts? Is this what you think this whole thing is about? Having doubts about God's love for me? See, having doubts means something is there before you but somehow, you don't just see and believe it. In my case, it isn't about doubts. It's about being realistic and facing the truth as it is. The reality is, I'm nothing but a bundle of shame and disappointment, and God doesn't spare as much as a glance for a lady. . ...."

"When you think of Peter, what comes to your mind?"

My friend cut me off.

"Peter?"

"Yes, Peter. The Head of the Church, the Rock on which Christ built his Church. When you think of him, what comes to your mind?"

Peter needed no introduction. A sculpture of him holding a bunch of keys still stands at the Basilica of the Most Holy Trinity, Onitsha and I often cracked jokes about meeting him at the gate of heaven and keeping watch with him so as to prevent some friends of mine from entering heaven.

However, for the first time in my life, I thought about him.

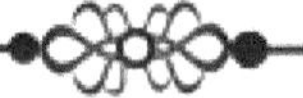

CHAPTER TWO

Simon Peter

"Even today, we are still so much closer to Peter in our flaws than his virtues, and Christ is still our rescue. May that never change. Amen".

- **Anonymous**

"Peter always made a fuss

Peter was impetuous

He knew hard times when he denied his Lord

But hardly had he fallen

When he sat right up began again

Christ named him the Rock,

As his reward".

These are the lyrics of an offertory hymn we sang during my days in the boarding school. We sang the hymn and we rose from our seats and walked to the offertory bucket into which we dipped our hands, dropped our offering and walked back to our seats. I also remember our school uniforms which doubled as our Sunday church wears.

As I focused on Peter that Saturday afternoon, these lyrics ran through my mind. I also remembered the times I did or said something right and my younger sister said,

'Chioma, flesh and blood didn't reveal this to you".

She was reminiscing the time Peter told Jesus he was the Son of the Living God and Jesus responded that flesh and blood didn't reveal that truth to him. (Matthew 16:13-20).

I remembered that shortly after the "flesh and blood" episode, Peter spoke out of turn, more like offered an unsolicited advice or sort of tried to be the "positive apostle" and Jesus rebuked him. (Matthew 16:21-23)

I remembered that I used to wonder how many blunders Peter committed which weren't captured in the Bible and if he had a wife and what living with him as a husband and a father felt like.

The more I thought of Peter, the more I wondered the nexus between Peter and I. Surely. Peter's daughter never got pregnant and disgraced him, and of course, Peter was a man so there was no way he could've taken in, unlike me who struggled with the reality of having a child and the circumstances that surrounded it.

"I don't think of Peter as a pillar of righteousness. I see him instead as an example of someone who was human and who received grace, mercy and help as many times as he failed."

- *Dominick Santore.*

My friend seemed to have read my mind for he rested his back on the sofa and spoke to me.

"I know a lot of pastors, priests and church leaders cite Peter as an example of who we shouldn't be or what we shouldn't do. We read the story of how he was the first to tell Jesus to ask him to come to him when He walked on the sea and they tell us to be a little discreet with our words. We read other stories of his and we are told we shouldn't be so sure, we shouldn't deny Jesus, we should stand and confess Jesus even when it's hard to do so and that we should be slow to speak and quick to listen. Nice homilies and messages, preaching and speeches, whatever you choose to call them. However, to me, Peter is and will always be a role model because reading about him tells me I'm not alone, that it's okay to be human and most importantly, being human with God actually gets rewarded".

I didn't understand what he meant by "being human with God actually gets rewarded" so I was quiet. My 2 months old baby slept beside me and I reached out and adjusted the wrapper and the baby pink shawl I covered him with.

> *"Immediately, Jesus made the disciples get into the boat and go on ahead of him to the other side, while he dismissed the crowd. After he had dismissed them, he went up on a mountainside by himself to pray. Later that night, he was there alone and the boat was already at a considerable distance from*

land, buffeted by the waves because the wind was against it. Shortly before dawn, Jesus went out to them, walking on the lake. When the disciples saw him walking on the lake, they were terrified.

"It's a ghost", they said and cried out in fear.

But Jesus immediately said to them.

"Take courage! It is I. Don't be afraid".

"Lord, if it's you", Peter replied, "Tell me to come to you on the water."

"Come", he said.

Then Peter got down out of the boat, walked on the water and came towards Jesus. But when he saw the wind, he was afraid and he began to sink and he cried out, "Lord save me".

Immediately, Jesus reached out his hand and caught him.

"You of little faith", he said. "Why did you doubt?".

(Matthew 14:22-31)

"This is one of the passages I love the most because I relate so much with it".

It was my friend and it turned out he had read from his phone. While he spoke, he fixed his gaze somewhere in front of him and I wondered if there was an invisible being he was staring at, someone from whom he took instructions. I also wondered what memories flooded his mind as he recalled the lessons he learnt from them.

"We can talk about Peter all we want. We can call him messy, impetuous and garrulous but the truth remains that we all sink like Peter. You, me, your parents, my mom, all of us, and the earlier we understood and embraced this truth, the better we'll learn to see that perhaps, the important message of that part of the bible isn't really about having an unwavering faith or a perfect faith. To me and I think it's true for us all, the important lessons of that story are: What Peter did when he began to sink and what Jesus did when Peter called out to him."

According to him, Peter stepped out of that boat with faith because well, Jesus called him to come. However, his faith wasn't perfect. It was faith sprinkled with a healthy dose of human nature, the kind of faith we are told we must never have. Peter stepped out of the boat and took steps on water, he noticed the violent wind around him.

"Chioma, that wind was real. When Peter noticed and became afraid of the fierce wind and the raging sea, he was being human. He was in full touch with his reality. Yes, Jesus knew about the wind, yet He asked him to come. Truth is, if Peter pretended it wasn't there and that he wasn't scared, he would've been in denial and plain delusional, and I don't think we are called to live in denial. In the same vein, your experience is real. Your pain and confusion is real. Look at your child who sleeps peacefully beside you. He is a full human who needs to be cared and provided for, and he is real. Therefore, those questions you ask in your heart are normal and completely valid.

To say the opposite is to encourage you to live in denial and that's not the reason I'm here."

As he spoke, I lowered my head and blinked severally to fight the tears. For the first time, no one forced motivational or inspirational quotes down my throat and someone let me know that how I felt was normal. For the first time, someone let me know that the doubts and the confusion I felt were normal and for the first time, there was enough space for me to feel. It was such a relief and I closed my eyes, and savored the peace and relief that flooded my heart.

"When Peter noticed the wind and began to sink, what did he do? Did he beat himself up for not being a true apostle of Jesus? Did he blame himself for noticing the wind and the sea, and not focusing on Jesus who called him? Did he convince himself that Jesus would be angry with him and recoil in his shame?"

"No". I shook my head.

"So what did he do? He reached out to Jesus and cried to be saved. He cried to Jesus as the human he was and he let Jesus know he needed help. This was what I meant when I said you should go to God in your doubts and with the hideous things you said about yourself. Most importantly, when Peter cried out to Jesus, what did Jesus do? How did he respond? Did he cuss him out for noticing the fierce wind instead of focusing on coming to him?"

"No".

"Did he laugh at him and make fun of him for being so weak when 'ordinary wind' almost caused him to sink to the bottom of the raging sea?"

"No".

"Did he say one word that suggested how disappointed he felt because Peter should've known and behaved better?"

"No".

"So what did he do? He reached out quickly, grabbed Peter's hand and pulled him from the sea. This is exactly what Jesus does when we come to him with our doubts, fears, questions and confusion, including those hideous words you uttered about yourself. He reaches out to you in your confusion and wavering faith, and he saves and rescues you. Again, I tell you, I didn't visit you today to tell you 'it's well' or some of those things people say. I've come to see how you are faring with your baby and to let you know that as confused and lost as you are, and as bad as you feel about yourself, you are human and it's completely normal. All I ask is that you remember to cry out and reach to God with those thoughts and feelings of yours. I know that Jesus who reached out quickly and grabbed Peter's hand will also reach out to you, grab your hand, pull you up and let you know how much He loves you."

By the time he let out the last word, I couldn't fight the tears anymore. I wailed and sobbed, and my shoulders heaved. It didn't matter to me that I would wake my son. All I wanted to do (and did) was cry as though I had been paid to do so.

I used to think I'd better keep
my eyes on Jesus or I'll drown.

My Goodness! What a burden to bear. I see it so differently now. I see Jesus walking on the water, Jesus calling Peter to come and Jesus rescuing Peter. Even when he said, 'Why did you doubt?' Jesus is grabbing hold of Peter and pulling him up.

- ***Dominick Santore***

My friend and I had one of the deepest conversations I've ever had in my life that Saturday afternoon and all these years, this conversation has occupied a special place in my heart. However, I didn't give myself a chance to express my doubts and confusion until 4 to 5 years later. When I did, I became a recipient of the compassion, mercy, grace and help that Peter received when he reached out to Jesus.

It wasn't sudden. It was gradual but God taught me and let me see I'm His daughter and there isn't a way to just stop loving me. He cleared my doubts and restored my faith in His love for me.

Thinking of my mom's experience, I now see that contrary to the words of Chidimma's mom, my mom didn't commit any sin and there was no need to confess to a priest. My mom asked those questions because her experience was real and she was human. Like Peter, everything she noticed, the people who would go hungry, the financial state of our home, the fear of starting afresh and the bulk purchases she made, were real.

She asked those questions because she needed to express her pain, confusion and doubts, and it didn't make her less a Christian. It didn't also mean she didn't know who God was.

Your shop may not have been ravaged by fire and you may not have handled the challenges I've handled. However, it's possible you've spent all you have on a sick family member or a loved one and still, you couldn't save him/her, and you are confused because you prayed and asked for quick recovery and divine healing.

Your family or marriage may be going through a rough time and deep inside you, you know how much you prayed, sought direction and discernment. You are wondering if you discerned properly, if God truly led you because there's just no way could God have led you into a disaster. It could be your business, your spouse, a particular sibling or a child of yours.

We can preach and tell ourselves to keep our eyes on Jesus, the author and finisher of our faith but if we are true to ourselves, we don't do this all the time.

None of us remembers to keep his/her eyes on Jesus at all times. Our eyes wander and they notice. Our heads turn and we can't help but take in the chaos and confusion that surrounds us. Our faith waver and shake.

Does it mean we are terrible Christians, bad people and weak followers of Christ?

No.

Instead, it means we are humans and we do nothing other than express our humanity. Luckily, our God understands this and doesn't condemn or blame us.

You don't have to recoil in shame when you feel confused or doubtful. You don't have to blame and condemn yourself for being a weak Christian and you don't have to visit any church to confess your sin of doubt.

You are only human and even in your fears, doubts and confusion, you deserve compassion, mercy, grace and help, and most importantly, God is always ready to listen and give you these gifts.

Like Peter did, reach out to Him.

CHAPTER THREE

Father of the Possessed

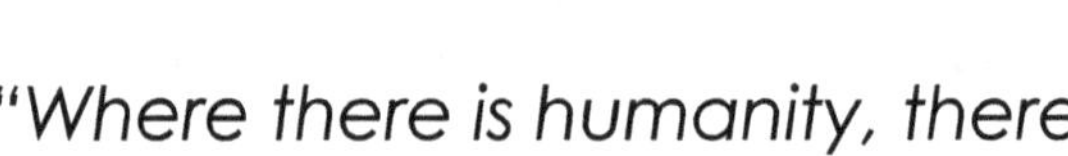

"Where there is humanity, there is doubt".

- **Stewart Stafford**

A lady was once approached by a young man who desired to court and marry her. He talked about the things he loved about her and he let her know he desired to make her his wife. The lady was quiet as she listened to him. All the while, she had just one question and when he exhausted his speech, she looked at him and said,

"You know, these words of yours sound familiar. A lot of men have said them to me and sadly, I found out that the lips which said these words weren't genuine. What makes you different? Why should I believe you?"

In other words, "I doubt it when you say you want me to marry you. I don't believe you because I've been lied to and taken for a ride, (possibly) jilted and treated badly by men. I find it difficult to believe you".

Surely, a lot of us have had our fair share of betrayal and lies from people we trusted so I think we can relate with this lady. These days, we have every reason to doubt the intentions of our friends, family members, even our spouses and parents, and the reason is simple: We've been hurt before and we don't want to be hurt again.

> *When He came to the other disciples, He saw a large crowd around them and the teachers of the law arguing with them.*

As soon as all the people saw Jesus, they were overwhelmed with wonder and ran to greet him.

"What are you arguing with them about?" he asked.

A man in the crowd answered,

"Teacher, I brought You my son, who is possessed by a spirit that has robbed him of speech. Whenever it seizes him, it throws him to the ground. He foams at the mouth, gnashes his teeth and becomes rigid. I asked your disciples to drive out the spirit, but they could not."

"You unbelieving generation," Jesus replied, "How long shall I stay with you? How long shall I stay with you? How long shall I put up with you? Bring the boy to me."

So they brought him. When the Spirit saw Jesus, it immediately threw the boy into a convulsion. He fell to the round and rolled around, foaming at the mouth.

Jesus asked the boy's father, "How long has he been like this?"

"From childhood", he answered. "It has often thrown him into fire or water to kill him. But if you can do anything, take pity on us and help us."

"If you can?" said Jesus.

"Everything is possible for one who believes."

Immediately, the boy's father exclaimed, "I do believe, help my unbelief!"

When Jesus saw that a crowd was running to the scene, he rebuked the impure spirit. "You deaf and mute spirit," he said, "I command you to come out

> *of him and never enter him again."*
>
> *The Spirit shrieked, convulsed him violently and came out. The boy looked so much like a corpse that many said, "He's dead". But Jesus took him by the hand and lifted him to his feet and he stood up."*
>
> - ***Mark 9:14-27 NIV***

The first thing that comes to mind after reading this story is similar to the things we've been taught about Peter and those days, I remember that I asked,

"Why exactly did you bring your son if you didn't believe Jesus could heal him?"

For others, the lesson could be about casting out a certain kind of demon and the importance of fasting. However, in recent times, I have read this story and understood it differently. For me, the most important lesson for me is about having doubts and what to do when the faith I have isn't enough.

As I imagine this father watching the disciples, the men who were close to the Teacher, as they made attempts to help his son, attempts which turned out to be futile, I see how his spirit must have fallen and his hopes dashed.

I remember my days as a mom to a five year old little boy. My son was ill and my mom called and informed me. I rushed to St. Charles' Borromeo Hospital Onitsha from my place of work and met my dad and my sick child. My son was weak, so weak that he couldn't even smile at me when he opened his eyes and saw me, and when I called his name and asked him to stay with mommy, he answered me but his voice was faint, like someone who answered from a distant place away from home.

We were taken to the emergency ward and a nurse was assigned to him. I watched as she fumbled with the syringe which was meant to be inserted into my son's arm and vein as a passage for the drip he was placed on. My son was weak but as the nurse fumbled with the syringe, he cried out in pain, his face turned red and all the veins in his neck became visible. Droplets of my son's blood graced the tiled floor of the ward and my heart shattered to pieces.

It didn't matter that my parents were there. I shouted at her to "Just stop hurting my son" and requested that another nurse be assigned to us. In fact, I ran out and spoke to a female doctor I met earlier who happened to be my primary school classmate. I pleaded with her to come and help us.

I think every parent can relate to this story. I'm a professional and I trained as a lawyer, and I think the story of the man whose son was possessed can be likened to submitting yourself to a younger doctor, attorney, solicitor or an intern who couldn't help you.

You are angry and hopeless, and you wonder what the younger professional has learnt from his senior colleague if he couldn't deliver on a 'simple job".

> *We look to the virtuous characteristics of the Old Testament saints and forget the shadier parts of their stories, or at least, we gloss over them and focus on the*

best parts. We forget David was a murderer, Noah, a drunk.

- ***Santore.***

I'm not sure of this father's expectations and how high they were but I'm sure they didn't include watching the futile attempts made by the disciples and watching as his son foamed through his mouth and rolled on the floor. Even when Jesus approached and the boy was brought to Him, instead of fleeing, the demon threw the boy into convulsion.

Taking all of these into consideration, surely you can understand how natural and human it was for the man to nurture some doubts in his heart.

I understand how he felt when he said, "If you can do anything, take pity on us and help us".

His doubt was understandable and if we are honest to ourselves, we have all been in situations where we felt powerless, helpless and heartbroken, and we wondered if God was near, if He could see and if He could hear.

We know we should have faith but at those times and moments, we just can't summon enough strength to proclaim what we believe in. We don't even know what to believe in anymore.

So what do we do?

Do we recoil and blame ourselves for not being a true christian and a gallant soldier and warrior?

I do believe. Help my unbelief

This was the father's response when Jesus picked on his expression of doubt, pointed out his lack of faith and taught him that "Everything is possible to him who has faith".

Another version of the bible reads,

I believe. Help my unbelief.

Yet another reads,

I have faith. Help my lack of faith.

In other words, the man says,

> *I know I don't have faith. My faith is far from being perfect. Please help me to have faith in you.*

An acknowledgement of his doubts and imperfection, and a genuine and total submission to He who can help him.

How did Jesus respond to his admission of doubts and genuine prayer for a stronger faith?

He didn't rebuke or scold or blame him. Instead, he moved on and granted healing to his son.

Truth is, we are imperfect humans and most times, our faith can be inadequate and easily overpowered by our present circumstances. If you find yourself with an imperfect, inadequate and overpowered faith, there is nothing wrong with you and there is nothing to be ashamed of.

Borrow this father's words.

Feel free to modify it slightly to suit whatever situation that has rendered your faith inadequate.

> *As always, we can ask for what we need. When we doubt, we can ask for more faith. When we are wavering*

in our resolve to follow, we can ask for more resolve.

- ***Anonymous***

Come as you are, with your inadequate faith. You have the perfect assurance that Jesus, who was human like you and I in every way yet without sin, and who understands, will help you and grant your prayers according to His will.

CHAPTER FOUR

Thomas

"Hope died. Faith died. I think it's safe to say that Thomas was hurt and of course, no one who believed and was hurt would like to believe again because believing again means exposing oneself to another hurt".

- **Anonymous.**

My elder brother and my sisters have had their fair share of being called "Bro Tom" or "Sister Tom". It was my way of calling them out when I tell them things and they express doubt. My son is also tired of retorting that his name isn't Thomas.

The story of Thomas, the apostle of Jesus who doubted His resurrection and appearance to his apostles reminds me of a story my maternal grandmother told me.

It was about a young man whose parent was ill. I'm not sure which of the parents now but a parent of his was ill. The young man sensed his parent would die so he told his people he wanted to travel to a faraway land. He told them he wouldn't return and they shouldn't send or look for him until something unusual happened.

The young man left his home to God-knows-where and shortly after he left, his parent passed away. His relatives came together in search of a way to bring the young man back home so he could face his responsibilities and lay his dead parent to rest. They sent several messages to him to come home and with each message the young man received, he responded with a simple question, "Has anything unusual happened?"

One can only imagine how frustrating it was for the young man's relatives.

They came together and searched for something unusual which might pique the young man's interest. Soon enough, they came up with something and then sent a message to the young man. They told him that a head of palm fruit ripened on a palm frond.

If you let out a laugh at this point, I won't blame you because knowing what a palm frond is and how heavy a head of palm fruit is, I laughed too when I heard this.

It was impossible but it was enough and turned out to be the exact message they needed to bring the young man home. The young man thought it was impossible. He said he needed to see what they were saying so he could believe.

So what did he do?

He left whatever he was doing wherever he was and returned home as quickly as he could and of course, when he returned, his relatives told him to face his responsibility and bury his dead parent.

The story was about shying away from responsibilities but I see a certain similarity between this young man and Thomas who was an apostle of Jesus. For Thomas and this young man, seeing was believing. They needed to see before they could believe.

Unless I see in his hands the mark of the nails and place my finger into the mark of the nails, and place my hand into his side, I will never believe.

- **John 20:24-29**

He was an apostle, he went everywhere with Jesus and listened to everything He said, including the times He prophesied about His death and resurrection.

However, I don't think Thomas and indeed any of His apostles knew and understood the depth of those prophesies and the extent of the suffering, humiliation and the kind of death their Teacher and Master would endure. Therefore, naturally when they witnessed his arrest, scourging, crucifixion and death, a lot of them including Thomas lost faith and most likely questioned themselves and asked the reason they even believed, trusted and followed him in the first place.

I don't blame them honestly.

This was a man who raised Lazarus even after he had been buried for three days and several other people, and surely, one would expect Thomas and other apostles to remember these events and believe that He who raised these people was also capable of raising himself.

Jesus' willingness to accommodate Thomas' unbelief is a reminder that God can handle our doubt.

- **David D. Flowers.**

Let's step into Thomas' shoes for a moment. Go with Jesus as He expressed sorrow and wept in front of the tomb of Lazarus and then asked him to "come out". Watch him as he felt compassion for the widow of Nain, raised her son from the dead and extended same grace and gesture to other people. Walk with Him as He healed the sick, including the soldier whose servant was ill and close to death, the one who told him he only needed to say a word and his servant would be healed, and feel the joy and the euphoria that enveloped you when you knew your Master was the center of attraction. Now, this master of yours who healed other people, no matter how bad and ugly their conditions were, and raised other people from death couldn't even save himself when his time came.

He said the Son of man would be glorified and yet you saw pieces of his flesh and splashes of his blood all over the place as he was scourged. You watched as he lifted his cross, fell three times and became so exhausted that someone had to be forced to help him lest he died, you watched as they stripped him of his clothes and made mockery of him and you heard his groans and cries as the nails cut through his veins and glued him to the cross. You watched him call out to God and ask why he had been forsaken, you watched him beg for drinking water and you watched as he breathed his last and you wonder if that was the glorification he meant.

What was glorifying about the most humiliating and painful death any human has ever been subjected to?

Suddenly, you who swelled with pride, joy and the euphoria of being with the Master and Teacher who was the center of attraction shrank in fear and apprehension and became afraid of being humiliated and killed.

Let's not forget that these apostles, including Thomas, left everything and followed Jesus. Sometimes I wonder and ask myself, "If these men knew and understood what Jesus meant when He said He would be glorified, if they knew that Jesus would be arrested, sentenced, scourged and crucified, would they have left everything and followed him everywhere?"

You see, it is very easy to read these stories and cast aspersions on Thomas for expressing doubts but when you step into his shoes for a moment, see everything he saw and feel everything he felt, you'll understand that any human in his place, including you and I, would be confused, afraid and filled with doubts.

> *The doubt Thomas experienced in the face of the heartbreaking loss of the one he loved and left everything to follow is like the doubt we feel when we face a massive loss, despair, heartbreak and sorrow, and Christ sympathizes with all of us.*
>
> - **Got questions ministries.**

I know for sure that I might not have been as blunt as Thomas was but I would have scoffed and shaken my head, rolled my eyes and told everyone off.

> *Eight days later, the disciples were in the house again and Thomas was with them. The doors were closed but Jesus came in and stood among them. "Peace be with you," he said. Then he spoke to Thomas, "Put your finger here. Look here are my hands. Give me your hand; put it into my side. Do not be unbelieving anymore but believe." Thomas replied, "My Lord and My God".*

> *"You believe because you can see. Blessed are those who have not seen and yet believe."*

No rebuke and no condemnation.

He simply called out to him to put his finger in the appropriate places. He led him from a place of doubt to a place where he had no choice but to profess his belief once again in the Lord he had known for years and the Lord he left everything to follow.

> *Let's remember that Jesus didn't leave Thomas to suffer without the blessing of faith and confidence; He gave him the*

evidence he required. That is typical of Jesus' approach to doubt; He responded to honest doubters in the way he knew best, the way that would help them to move from doubt to knowledge.

- **Dallas Willard**

One of my favourite quotes is,

If the spark is so bright, what must be the flame? If the human love thrills me so, what must be the heart of God?"

I read it from one of my favourite authors then, Archbishop Fulton Sheen. I think the title of that book of his was "You" and I remember he said that love, genuine care and kindness, and all the good qualities we have felt and experienced from our loved ones are nothing but tiny reflections of the ultimate source of all good things, God.

According to him, if you think your mom is so kind, your dad is so caring and your friend is so warm and a great and patient listener who understands and picks you up, have you ever taken the time to think and reflect on how much more God who created these loved ones of yours and who is the source of these good qualities they embody? Have you ever wondered how caring, kind, patient and loving He is?

I completely agree with him and each time I'm offered help, forgiveness, grace, understanding, compassion and kindness, I am reminded of God who is the source of these good qualities I have experienced and I know He is even kinder, more caring and compassionate and deeply forgiving.

We are not perfect. We quarrel with our parents, spouses and children. We do things we don't want to do and we don't do things we want to do. Yet, even when we are angry and not talking to our loved ones, we still see them.

We see what they don't show us, we hear what they don't say and we know what they feel and even feel with them. We hear their voices on the phone and sense their pain and sometimes, when they rant, shout and scream, we don't retaliate because we know they are simply reacting to pain or fear. The love we have for them enables us to see beyond certain flaws and attitudes of theirs and connect with their pain, fear or their deep feelings.

In the same way, God sees us. He saw the pain, grief, fear and hopelessness behind Thomas' doubts and He sees the pain, grief and fear behind the doubt we feel.

He doesn't leave us in our doubt. No. Instead, He leads us gently, compassionately, tenderly and lovingly from our doubt to faith and hope.

He knows all things and He knows the doubts you nurture in your heart so you don't have to hide them from Him.

Go to Him as you are and let Him take your hand and reassure you that He can be trusted.

CHAPTER FIVE

God rewards doubt

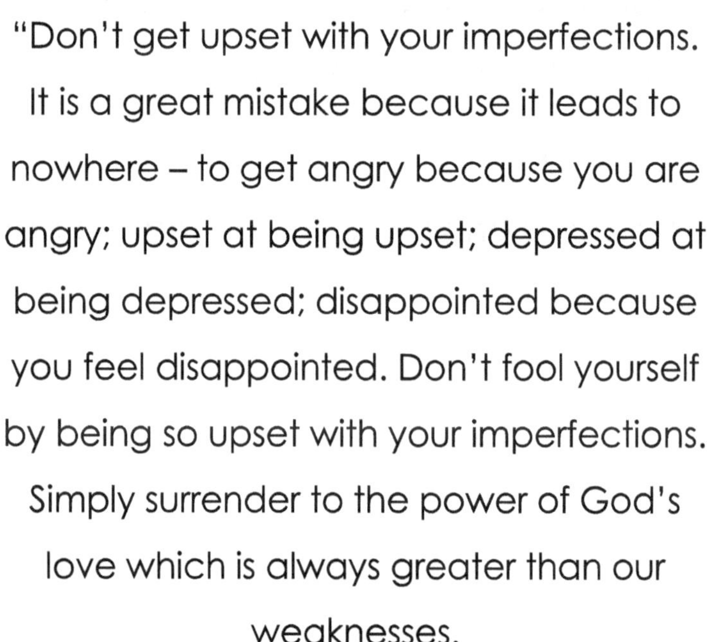

"Don't get upset with your imperfections. It is a great mistake because it leads to nowhere – to get angry because you are angry; upset at being upset; depressed at being depressed; disappointed because you feel disappointed. Don't fool yourself by being so upset with your imperfections. Simply surrender to the power of God's love which is always greater than our weaknesses.

- **Francis De Sales**

I've heard the clause, "to fulfil all righteousness" so often that it has become a cliché. Recently, a colleague of mine said he needed to "fulfil all righteousness" about a work related issue and for the first time in years, I thought of its origin.

"John the Baptist said this in the bible right?"

My colleague searched my face.

"Hanty, when was the last time you read your bible? It was Jesus Christ please. He said it shortly before John the Baptist baptized him."

I rolled my eyes while other staff giggled.

"At least, I know it had something to do with John the Baptist and Jesus Christ during the baptism of Jesus, and there was no need to throw shades."

I rolled my eyes again.

I was right, at least 80%. It was during the baptism of Jesus. According to the bible, Jesus came to John to be baptized and knowing who Jesus was, John refused at first and told Jesus he was unfit to baptize him. Jesus answered, "Let it be so now; it is proper for us to do this to fulfil all righteousness". Then John baptized Jesus.

John was present when the Spirit of God descended on Jesus like a dove and a voice from heaven proclaimed Jesus as the beloved son of God (Matthew 3:17). As a foetus in the womb of his mother, Elizabeth, John leapt with joy at the presence of Christ who was also growing in the womb of his mother, Mary and it was John who proclaimed that Jesus was the "Lamb of God who takes away the sins of the world".

He made it clear that Jesus was the one he spoke of when he said, "He who comes after me has surpassed me because he was before me" and he let people know that Jesus was the Messiah.

Yet, while he was in prison, held captive by Herodias and awaiting execution, he called two disciples of his and requested that they go to Jesus and ask,

> *Are you the one who is to come, or shall we look for another?* (Matt 11:3, Lk 7:19)

Seriously?

"John, you of all people? After everything you've seen, heard and testified about Jesus? If you weren't sure, why did you point him out to people as the Lamb of God and the one who comes after you and who surpassed you? Can you hear yourself now? Why would you even let yourself succumb to this level of doubt?"

There is but just one answer to these questions.

John was human and at the point he sent those men to ask that question, he was being what we all are, human.

> *Each time I reflect on John's doubt, it gives me a certain freedom; the freedom from the shame of admitting the doubt I feel.*
>
> - ***Shelby Abbot***

He was in his dark times, stuck and alone in a filthy prison with no hope of release in sight and of course, it was natural to be overwhelmed by his own thoughts.

It is possible John knew Jesus was the Messiah but he just needed to hear it again, a kind of reassurance. It's possible he knew his end was near and he wanted to be sure he hadn't unleashed a false prophet on the people he once preached to. It's also possible he wondered the reason Jesus didn't come for him and save him, that is if he was truly the Messiah.

I'm not a bible scholar and I'm not sure of the thoughts John had in his mind at the time he sent those disciples to Jesus but one thing was certain; John wasn't just sure anymore and there were doubts in his mind.

In the same way, most of us aren't just sure anymore. Times are tough and some of us have lingering doubts in our mind, thoughts that have refused to go away despite the many times we have failed to acknowledge them.

Now, how did John handle the doubt he felt about Jesus?

He simply reached out to Jesus through his disciples and asked for clarification. He asked questions and of course, he got answers that kept him at peace. Jesus met his doubt with answers.

> *Go back and tell John what you hear and see, the blind see again and the lame walk,*

> *those suffering from virulent skin-diseases are cleansed and the deaf hear, the dead are raised to life and the good news is proclaimed to the poor. Blessed is anyone who does not stumble on account of me.*

More so, Jesus went ahead to say things about John which tells me that John's expression of doubt didn't affect the way Jesus saw him.

> *God desires our belief (faith) but He also welcomes our confusion.*
>
> - **Barnabas Piper**

God rewards our doubt with answers, clarity and peace. He knows what we are made of, He remembers we are dust and He knows we will stumble and experience dark times in our journeys so our doubts don't surprise him.

Feel your doubts and express them.

Someone once said that God is God all by himself and that He isn't affected or diminished by the questions we ask him or the doubts we express.

I agree with her.

- It is human to doubt;
- An expression of doubt doesn't make you less a christian; and

- Jesus welcomes those doubts and rewards them with clarity and peace.

HE UNDERSTANDS…

Father, if you are willing, take this cup away from me. Nevertheless, let Your Will be done, not mine.

Lk 22:41-42.

At the time He made this statement, it was recorded that Jesus was in anguish and that in His anguish, he prayed more earnestly and His sweat fell to the ground like great drops of blood.

I'm sure that if his apostles hadn't been asleep and had observed Jesus more closely, they would have noticed he was (most likely) sweating on his palms and that his body shook.

In this case, it wasn't doubt. It was fear.

Jesus knew what would happen to him. He knew all along that he would be glorified and he even prophesied about it and rebuked Peter who once tried to talk him out of it.

However, few hours to his glorification, his humanity took over. He became afraid of what he would face and how much he would suffer, the same way we have felt afraid one time or the other.

Like doubt, fear is another feeling that makes us human and each time I think about the prayer of Jesus in the garden of Gethsemane, I am reminded of the popular gospel artiste, Don Moen, and one of his songs, "God with us".

He walked where I walk (x2)
He stood where I stand (x2)
He felt what I feel (x2)
He understands.

He knows my frailty (x2)
Shared my humanity (x2)
Tempted in everywhere (x2)
Yet without sin

God with us,
So close to us,
God with us,

Emmanuel.

I am also reminded of that portion of the Bible which encourages us to approach God's throne with confidence and seek mercy and grace when we need them because we have a high priest who understands our humanity. (Hebrew 4:15-16)

> *God already knows my future and in His plans for me, He made room for my weaknesses.*
>
> - ***Toluwanimi Lazarus.***

At all times, whether we feel afraid or doubtful, God understands. Jesus sees and He knows the feeling. He is ever ready to provide help, support and comfort as we journey through life.

I'm rooting for you always,

Chioma.

www.ingramcontent.com/pod-product-compliance
Lightning Source LLC
LaVergne TN
LVHW050318160826
845677LV00014B/3458
* 9 7 8 9 7 8 8 4 1 5 9 2 3 *